Invisible Harvest

by
Thomas John Carlisle

Photographs by
Dorothy Mae Carlisle

GRAND RAPIDS, MICHIGAN
WILLIAM B. EERDMANS PUBLISHING COMPANY

Dedicated
to
our four beloved sons:

Thomas Dwight Carlisle
Christopher Davis Carlisle
David Livingstone Harold Carlisle
Jonathan Tristram Carlisle

Copyright © 1987 by Wm. B. Eerdmans Publishing Co.
255 Jefferson Ave. S.E., Grand Rapids, Mich. 49503
Printed in the United States of America

Library of Congress Cataloging-in-Publication Data
Carlisle, Thomas John.
Invisible harvest.
I. Title.
PS3553.A7315   1987   811'.54   87-27323
ISBN 0-8028-0274-5

Preface

The words "invisible harvest" are a paradox but a fruitful one. In my poem of that title the reader discovers (as do I, the poet) that the harvest of that summer's day is much more than the succulent blackberries.

The third line enunciates a superior harvest, "fragile fruits of silence"—the solitude and time for meditation that all of us need and find so hard to come by. Near the end of the poem there is the indication that we may need to bleed literally or figuratively as part of sustaining a complete life.

The poem makes consistent use of the slant rhyme so characteristic of Emily Dickinson. This also says something about the unevenness of life in a way that adds to the poem's richness.

A book of poetry would seem to be a *visible* harvest—in this instance, of my lifework. But the invisible aspects of the poems themselves are what constitute the greater harvest. "The things which are seen are temporal; the things which are unseen are eternal," as Paul reminds us.

To enjoy the harvest of poetry, one needs to look not only at the visible poem but at its less visible aspects and its invisible ones as well. This takes time. It involves reading aloud. It requires coming back to the poem a number of times. And for all this, there is a reward. There *is* a harvest.

A poem does not have to be directed to a harvest, but I am surprised to find that a number of my poems are exactly that. Look at the poems in Section I, for example. "Field at Arles" has its "sea of burning grain" leading to the inexplicable gateway to knowledge. The children on a hill in "Far" are garnering their harvest of the world's mystery and wonder. The small boy with his rake in "Springtime in Autumn" is working with fall leaves, but his energies speak of spring and the future he may achieve. "Angelus at Auvers" is directly concerned with a literal harvest, but the Angelus, from the church tower in the distance, chimes of something much, much more. Even "Nativity" can be related to this basic idea.

As you proceed with the book, you will come to the enchanted land of the poet's harvest of words, the intricate harvest of our human psychology, the sowings and reapings of succeeding generations, the harvest of my wife's garden and her autumn leaves, Emily Dickinson's gathering of words, the oceanic harvest of the Nova Scotia fisherfolk, the harvest of our nation's sins as well as its indomitable spirit, the cidery harvest of Alfred Moon, and the harvest of our advancing years.

This book is a harvest, yet I hope it will be not an ending but a beginning, and that these words will continue to flourish and to grow as they are read and re-read, heard and re-heard.

The sound and meaning and nuances of words are to be melded with your own experiences and memories. So there is a way in which the book is to be a planting and a cultivating as well as a harvest. (If some of you want to hear my interpretation of the poems, audiotapes and videotapes will be available from me at our home at 437 Lachenauer Drive, Watertown, N.Y. 13601.)

Through the more than fifty years of our marriage—and in the seven-and-a-half years of our courtship—Dorothy Mae Davis, who became Dorothy Mae Carlisle, has expressed her creativity by composing pictures—with her camera. For a long time I have wished that some of them could be included in my books of poetry.

For the first time—in this, my eleventh book—I am delighted to be able to incorporate some of her pictures. She is accustomed to color photographs, but the exigencies of publishing require that all but the cover photograph be published here in black and white. Look at each picture for what it may have to offer you, just as you would peruse an individual poem.

These poems were selected from the work of all my years, although most of them were written in the last thirty-three years. It would have been pleasant to include one or two early childhood poems, or the Flag Day poem published in the *Plattsburgh Daily Republican* when I was ten, or "Save Old Ironsides," an irregular ode which I wrote when I was twelve. The following year I traveled to Washington, D.C., to recite it at a national convention of the Children of the American Revolution.

At commencement at Plattsburgh High School in 1930, I spoke on the importance of poetry. At Williams College I did honors work in American and British poetry and was a member of the editorial board of the literary magazine, *Sketch,* which published many of my poems. At Williams I was the first undergraduate to receive academic credit for creative writing.

It was not until I attended the University of New Hampshire Writers Conference in 1954 that I began to devote time each week to writing poetry and to submitting poems persistently to national publications. Although I suffered many rejections, I was rewarded with numerous acceptances, and through the years the number of my poems published has grown to well over one thousand in over 150 publications.

My first book was *My Names Are Different*—in 1957. Seven other books are noted in the Acknowledgments. Other significant poems are found in *You! Jonah!* (1968) and *Beginning with Mary* (1986).

Inevitably this new book had to be painfully selective—a sampling of my lifetime love of creative writing.

Invisible Harvest is a title both pregnant and poignant. I leave it to you to delve into the harvests, both visible and invisible, of this book.

Thomas John Carlisle

Appreciation

To so many people I am lovingly indebted for inestimable help and encouragement on my poetic journey. Here I shall attempt to name only some of those who are no longer in this world but whose inspiration continues to beacon me: Ruby Grace Carlisle, Thomas Houston Carlisle, Lillian Pike Everest, Helen E. Hale, Samuel Allen, Mary Ely Lyman, Loring Williams, John Holmes, and Calvin Bulthuis.

Those who have assisted me through their comments on this present manuscript include Dorothy M. Carlisle, Joan Donovan, James Dowd, Leonard J. Meinhold, Rev. Dr. Christopher D. Carlisle, Rev. Jonathan T. Carlisle, Rev. David L. H. Carlisle, María L. Carlisle, Kimberly Carlisle, David Ross Reid, and Elizabeth Carlisle Lewis. Mary Hietbrink has been both perceptive and supportive as my editor.

Especially I thank William B. Eerdmans, Jr., whose encouragement, humor, and wisdom have been a determinative factor in the publication of this and six earlier books.

Contents

Preface   *iii*

Appreciation   *v*

Acknowledgments   x

I. Invisible Harvest   1

Invisible Harvest   3
Field at Arles   4
Far   4
Lullaby in Gray   5
Inklings of Infinity   5
In That Garden   6
November Sunset   7
Springtime in Autumn   8
Angelus at Auvers   8
Nativity   9

II. Continually We Devise   11

Improvisations   12
For the Best Secrets   12
Again to Sonnets   13
Far Music   14
When My Heart Really Has Something to Say   14
Genius at Work   15
On Discovering and Recovering a Poem by Richard
    Crashaw   16
Number Five   17
A Separate Page   18
Right Moment   19
The Living Word   19

III. Making Our Way   21

Could I?   22
Portrait   23
Some of My Best Friends Are Doctors   24
After the Operation   26
At the Lunch Counter   27

Marilyn   29
Such a Tide   30
Re-Entry   31
Without a Question Mark   33
Under the Sign of Thomas   34
My Names Are Different   35
To See and Follow   36
A Light to Bring Us Safe   36
How Do You Patch Your Faith?   37

IV. Ascendants and Descendants   39

Ascendants   40
My Mother's Jewelry Box   41
My Father's House   42
Celebration of Love   42
Last Rites   43
A Name   44
Hello, Me   45
As a Little Child   46
With Tiny Hands   47
My Son   48
Our Mutual Friend   49
A Father to Me   50
Home   51

V. Rise Up, My Love, My Fair One   53

Keepsake   54
This New Word   55
The Little Girl You Were   56
The Sands of Dawn   57
In the Garden   57
November Night   58
New Bride   58
In the Thousand Islands   59
My Song of Songs   59
Every Time and Every Where   60
Rise Up, My Love, My Fair One   61
Ad Infinitum   61

VI. The Woman with the Perfect Word   63

Emily Dickinson   64
Since Emily Was Fond of God   64
Restoration   65
Emily Dickinson and the "Burglar"   65
"Mine by the Right of the White Election"   66
Emily Dickinson and Her "Burglar, Banker, Father"   67
The Handwriting of Emily Dickinson   67
A Miser's Privilege   68
In Manuscript   69
Before the Guests Arrive   70
Window to World   70
Well-Versed   71

VII. On the Shores of Nova Scotia   73

Necessary Maintenance   74
Returning   75
Voyager   76
A Taste for Tempest   76
A Metaphor for All Who Love the Sea   77
Good Morning   78
Invitation   79
Beacon   79
Ship-Fellow   80
Personal Geology   80
Hibernative   81

VIII. Part of a Purpose   83

People Part of a Purpose   84
Domestic Correspondence Two Days before Bunker Hill   87
From the Grave of a Revolutionary Soldier at Williamsburg   88
Sign Here   89
A Severe Struggle   90
Re-Crossing Brooklyn Ferry   91
Hosannas in the Forest   93
Remembering Hiroshima and Nagasaki   94
Destruction to the Nth Power   95
A Matter of Morals   96
Build Me a Shelter   96
America Dawn   97

IX. Our Jeopardy   103

    Our Jeopardy   104
    Through Cross Country   105
    When Age Enmeshes Me   106
    Retrieval System   106
    Requisition   107
    Almost Inaudible   108
    Moon Song   109
    Adelia Moon   110
    The Tragedy of Attrition   112
    Golden Hour   113
    A Touch of Autumn   113
    As Long as I Can   114
    All Is Safely Gathered   114
    Isaac and Rebecca   115
    Prospect   116

Acknowledgments

The author wishes to thank the following publications, in whose pages certain of these poems first appeared, for permission to include them in this book:

alive now!: "November Sunset," "Our Mutual Friend," "A Taste for Tempest," "Through Cross Country"

American Weave: "Angelus at Auvers," "From the Grave of a Revolutionary Soldier at Williamsburg"

Berkshire Review: "Moon Song," "Isaac and Rebecca"

California State Poetry Quarterly: "Such a Tide," "A Miser's Privilege"

Channels: "My Song of Songs," "Ad Infinitum"

Chicago Tribune: "Invisible Harvest," "Almost Inaudible"

Christian Century: "After the Operation," "Since Emily Was Fond of God," "Restoration," "Emily Dickinson and the 'Burglar,'" "A Severe Struggle"

Christian Herald: "As a Little Child," "Prospect"

Christian Science Monitor: "Field at Arles," "Far," "In That Garden," "Right Moment," "Ascendants," "Hello, Me," "With Tiny Hands," "The Sands of Dawn," "Emily Dickinson," "Necessary Maintenance," "Ship-Fellow," "Domestic Correspondence Two Days before Bunker Hill," "Golden Hour," "A Touch of Autumn"

Denver Post Empire Magazine: "Home"

Episcopalian: "The Living Word" "When Age Enmeshes Me," "Retrieval System"

Flame: "Build Me a Shelter"

Good Housekeeping: "Springtime in Autumn," "Sign Here"

Gospel Herald: "In the Garden"

Horn Book Magazine: "Improvisations," "Far Music," "The Little Girl You Were"

Kansas City Star: "Requisition," "As Long as I Can"

Ladies' Home Journal: "A Light to Bring Us Safe"

New England Quarterly: "Returning"

New Mexico Quarterly: "Lullaby in Gray"

New York Herald Tribune: "A Separate Page," "My Names Are Different," "A Name," "My Son"

New York Times: "All Is Safely Gathered"

Poetry Digest: "When My Heart Really Has Something to Say"

Presbyterian Life: "Could I?" "Re-Entry," "Under the Sign of Thomas," "Hosannas in the Forest," "America Dawn"

Presbyterian Survey: "The Tragedy of Attrition"

Purpose: "A Matter of Morals"

Rotarian: "My Mother's Jewelry Box," "Celebration of Love," "Last Rites," "A Father to Me," "Adelia Moon"

Seed: "The Handwriting of Emily Dickinson"

Theology Today: "Our Jeopardy"
Time of Singing: "Genius at Work"
Together: "Nativity"
Watertown Daily Times: "To See and Follow," "In the Thousand Islands,"
"Remembering Hiroshima and Nagasaki"
Yankee: "This New Word"

Some of these poems first appeared in earlier books by the author:

Eve and After (1984): "Every Time and Every Where," "Rise Up, My
Love, My Fair One"
I Need a Century (1963): "Again to Sonnets," "Without a Question Mark"
My Names Are Different (1957): "Inklings of Infinity," "Keepsake"
Tales of Hopkins Forest (1984): "People Part of a Purpose"

Several of the poems were reprinted in some of the foregoing books or in
Celebration! (1970), *Mistaken Identity* (1973), *Journey with Job* (1976), or
Journey with Jonah (1984).

"Rise Up, My Love, My Fair One" with music by Dr. Arthur W. Fracken-
pohl of Crane Music School has been published as a choir anthem and as a
solo by Shawnee Press, Delaware Water Gap, Pa.

Some of these poems have been reprinted in my monthly articles on
"Poetry for the Preacher" in *Church Management—The Clergy Journal,* and
others in the *Watertown* (N.Y.) *Daily Times* Sunday edition under the caption
"North Country Poet."

Harvest scene in Jefferson County, New York

I

Invisible Harvest

Invisible Harvest

My fingers are all purple
replenishing my pail
with fragile fruits of silence
today available.

I nibble at a berry
and savour its extent
while stripping bare the parent branch
for future sustenance.

I take no notice of the bell
that calls the town to noon.
I disregard the honeyed song
of bees in unison.

The thorn's rubescent comment
intrinsic to my need.
Invisible my harvest
but by it I am fed.

Field at Arles
(After Van Gogh)

I walked in the field of Arles
in a sea of burning grain.
A storm was alive in heaven
and my heart held a hurricane.

At the calm center of wonder
beside the cedars of awe
the mountains answered with thunder.
I trembled at what I saw.

For the law was written plainly
in green and bronze and blue
and what no one could explain to me
in that clear moment I knew.

Far

Far shall the children look and far
far shall the children see.
The afternoon has opened
a book of mystery
and wonder and all eloquent
sounds of the drowsing day.
And who shall say what the children know
or know what the children say?

Lullaby in Gray

dust
slowly
dust slowly
dust slowly gathers
gathers grows grips
the surface
gleamless
grayly spurns sunlight
spurns wonder
copies color
claims top more than sides
more than under
dust slowly
slowly dust
gathers grows gleamless
slowly slowly
dust

Inklings of Infinity

I should not say I know so much
    but only that I know.
The sky has reservoirs in space
    I gather from the snow.
Though never a star has fallen on me
    my uncomplaining eye
finds inklings of infinity.
    I know there is a sky.

In That Garden

There will be apples to eat in that garden
and we shall sit and talk and rise and choose
which shall be ours. Neither permission nor pardon
will be required. But we will use
more wisdom and clearer love than heretofore.
We shall spend the endless afternoon
listening to music and answering the troubadour,
and unwrapping the butterfly from his cocoon,
and asking the eagle what he sees from a throne
higher than ours, and probing deep
as to why sometimes even lovers must be separate and alone
and why the alertest must find time to sleep.

November Sunset

There will always be a sunset
so I do not need to run
to the window of my study
to enjoy the present one.

Yet there'll never be another
quite identical to this
so I stop my busy fingers
lest the beauty I should miss.

As I glory in its magic
and the scenes it paints for me
I should never take for granted
that tomorrow I can see.

So the sunset I am watching
on this brisk November night
is my foretaste and my promise
of the everlasting light.

Springtime in Autumn

Leaves laugh at the small boy.
His tall rake no tool but a toy.

He holds the tines in his hand
and drags the handle along the land.

No pyramid of leaves will rise
from his undirected energies.

No bonfire of his will blaze
and blend its smoke with autumn haze.

But in this season of harvesting
he is the one sure sign of spring.

Angelus at Auvers
(After Van Gogh)

The hay is stacked at Auvers and the brown
tumult admonishes the earlier green.
The bastioned church is waiting in the town
for harvest meditated but unseen.
This Angelus sounds only to the ear
according with the culminated sight
while mordant pigment melds the atmosphere
in unity of labor and delight.

8

Nativity

I did not see
the snow start.
It was all about me
before I bothered
to look out
my insulated
window.
Quieter than I
and willing
to work in small
crystallizations,
it set me
thinking of One
who comes
in minimal
but basic
terms.

*Potter James Kempes at work at Ghost Ranch, Abiquiu,
New Mexico*

II

Continually We Devise

Improvisations

Our lines are untidy mixtures of the strange,
the sordid, and the starless—and the starred.
We ourselves are not likely to change
but we ponder, erase, alter, discard
and devise. Continually we devise
and improvise improvidently. See,
we say, see with the stigmata of my eyes
how the image of the world appears to me.
Hear the music I have almost heard.
Taste the almost true—the almost living—word.

For the Best Secrets

My friend the poet used to rise and write
after the house had fallen all asleep.
The best way for the best secrets to keep
is to put them on paper in the night.
They are more luminous then. And halos hang
above folks whose character by day
appears to have them headed the other way.
What horns we summon up of *auld* and *lang*.
Dim words and signs that never think to burn
under the sun jump headlong when the still
of stars and slumber gives them free and will.
My little lantern allows me to discern
over the hill and farther than the best
of telescopes while others are at rest.

Again to Sonnets

Again to sonnets I might turn my hand
but hands are made to hold, to build, to give
shape to the shapeless, coin to the reft friend.
To hold a pencil to make the heart live
is almost much too much to make demand.
Fugitive I and undemonstrative
deny solicited and disciplined,
prefer straight jigger of perhaps and if.
So pattern shades to an unlikely shape,
a Rorschach blot upon an empty wall
past which a burst of meaning may escape,
a jagged window unconventional,
symmetric only to dimensionless
eyes stretched stretched stretched to clear sightedness.

Far Music

I dream far melody sublimely played
as darkness takes possession of my eyes.
Silent I am and sad but unafraid
because the dancer on the wire flies
across the night across the ocean and
sings in a town somewhere southwest in Spain.
And I awake in an enchanted land
where harvest needs no hand to sow the grain.

When My Heart
Really Has Something to Say

I would as soon compose my poetry
upon a computer as I would think
of dipping my finger into a bottle of ink
and tracing out my fancies nakedly.
Let me grip a pen or pencil in my hand
and set it moving in my own strange script:
the point shall become luminously tipped
and visit realms of an enchanted land.

Yet when my heart really has something to say,
shall I not take the nearest instrument,
carve words with stone or with the wayward juice
of berries wild until the thought I meant
is captured where upon some duller day
it will be ready to read and reproduce?

Genius at Work

How did Will Shakespeare feel whenever he
released immortal words until they shone?
Did even his pen hold radiance of its own
quiet upon his desk in reverie
of revelation? Mortal mystery
that one hears whispers in the dark alone
of all the hidden symbols he has known,
whispers which press the right to speak and be.
Did he believe and say, "This is my best,"
or did he rise, tired, disconsolate;
blow out the candle, struggle down the street;
and in the tavern join the raucous rest,
convinced that words meet such untimely fate
as ciphers tallied on time's balance sheet?

On Discovering and Recovering a Poem by Richard Crashaw (*c. 1613-1649*)

Long ago
the poem
was wrapped
in words.
Today
I take it
from its
swaddling cloths
and spread
its sounds
and symbols
to the sun
and feel
its flesh
and figures
with my fingers
and hold
its pith
and promise
and dream
some of the dreams
the poet made.

Number Five

William Carlos
Williams created
a red fire truck
with such fidelity
and force
and vision
that Charles Demuth
the poet's quiet friend
caught the careening
vehicle in bright
climactic circles—
what Hyatt Major calls
the *visual
equivalent*—
on brilliant canvas
with retreating
golden 5's
rushing to rescue
some home
or wharf
or warehouse
from the fury
of care-less flames
precipitating
night's incandescence.

The poem relates to William Carlos Williams' poem "The Great Figure" and the painting *I Saw the Figure Five in Gold* by Charles Demuth as explicated by A. Hyatt Major in *The Metropolitan Museum of Art: Favorite Paintings* (1979).

A Separate Page

When the book came unbound
and left me a separate page,
there were strange words I found,
my private heritage.

Even as the sun unset
touched me at evening's rim
my lips and eyes were met
by scarlet seraphim.

My health was in the red
liquor flowing through
my heart and around my head
and in the fragrant new

air that I imbibed
from tanks of borrowed sky.
O remedy prescribed,
I need a century.

Right Moment

Return in another season and we may
accept this word from you. Not now. Not now.
Perhaps it is perfect and should be kept
today. Possibly its meaning will grow
on both of us. There is no explaining moods:
yours that provoked the symbol, ours that turned
it aside as gray or bizarre. Some goods
grow brighter. Time finds what was earlier earned.
Ready—not ready. Count again to ten
before you start looking where the player hides.
Again. Start again. And again. And again.
And again. And you will be there when truth collides
with that impact devoid of fear or caution
that sets an imperial galaxy in motion.

The Living Word

I have rejoiced in words
their nuances
their honey and their tart
their sounds which bless my silence
and such utterance
as stirs my heart.

Without them I am crippled
deaf and blind
and all my hope is blurred
even as I find
no life   no joy   no love
without the living Word.

The Shenandoah at flood stage near Strasburg, Virginia

III

Making Our Way

Could I?

How would I manage
if the woe I see
others enduring
were to mangle me?
How handle the horror
of a damaged child
a cancered parent
or a death prescribed
for soldier son
or suicided friend
or bloody accident
of earth or sky?
How meet the musts
that woe upon the world:
the bombed the poisoned
and the meager fed?
The Jobs who have no tally
of their innocence
or their benevolence?
And Job's less righteous
brothers and sisters
in the human snarl
who cannot correlate
their doom with their deserving?
I think my lips
would stumble if I tried
to equate my natal nakedness
with stripped misfortune
or to balance
God's giving and God's taking.
Could I still
retrieve the *nonetheless* of faith
and say
I bless God?
Could I?

Portrait

Who disobeyed the doctor's word
of care of pulse or knee
or cast or detour of the heart's
revised anatomy

Who slaved till midnight drank past dawn
and chatted half the day
reined household but ironically—
himself the runaway

Who sidestepped love except when pain
prevented his resist
Of travel lover victim both
Whom death six times has kissed

Found refuge in the woods and went
where guidance has its fee
but ends when game is ferried home
He dreams that he is free

not free of love for there are those
who love him nonetheless
All roam   No rest   Imprisoned in
his private wilderness

Some of My Best Friends Are Doctors

My God
we expect the doctor
to be God
and forgive all our iniquities
heal all our diseases
crown our life with kindness
when he cannot manage
his own warts—
or she as the case may be.

We want the doctor
to be
our fortune-teller
our clairvoyant
and read our minds
and our meters
and scan our hidden parts
for malignancies
as well as find miracle cures
so we will be all well
in the morning.

We like to think
our beloved physician
received A plus
in every course
and maintains a hot line
to health and happiness.

We would pay
our practitioner
any amount
(or ask our medical
to cover it)
if that would only insure us
against every trace
of trouble
every particle
of pain
and the sure encroachment
of age and the undertaker.

Despite the degrees
and diplomas
(all over the wall)
and his—or her—
stethoscope diplomacy
we are suspicious
that our existential questions
will continue to go
unanswered.

Who will deliver us
from the body of this death
and the death of this body?
My God!

After the Operation

I have not forgotten
everything. I remember
that I am here
or an unreasonable
facsimile of me
looks listens and goes on
breathing as usual.
But there are blanks
holes in my memory
pages pasted shut
images torn or erased.
I claw at what is left
groping to retrieve
by sweat or association
my diminished soul
and its covenant allies.
If only I had an inkling
of what temporarily
or longer I have lost.
It is the mass of it
that frightens
                    alarms
                              terrifies.
Is there a resurrection
for mislaid thoughts and departed
dreams? I would answer
an advertisement
for such a miracle.

At the Lunch Counter

Sitting at the lunch
counter I listen
while the waitresses
deliver little
orders of gossip
and grief and anger
en route to tables
where untender mates
stir the vichyssoise
of incipient
misunderstandings.
Impotent salesmen
discuss their despairs
and secretaries
tear apart their sweet
Simon Legrees and try
to capture the eye
of the absorbed boys
arguing in the
next booth. I cannot
hear what the lovers
are thinking. I see
their carefully masked
faces. I shudder
at the blonde mother's
rude expectations
of her four-year-old
daughter exploring
the mysterious
menu and pounding
her spoon on the top
of the table and
spilling the water
on the no longer
clean red tablecloth.

The single student
cares more for her book
than her tossed salad.
The whole world is here
seen but unhearing
revealing feelings
and concealing at
the same time while I
must be something more
than anonymous
diner observer.
I must put my own
silver straight, empty
my plate which starving
souls would easily
envy, and ask for
dessert and coffee
and see to the check
and leave my correct
tip and re-enter
the night which I share
with hundreds hungry
for the nourishment
of companionship
and understanding
and one welcome word.

Marilyn

Waif
wishing to be
woman
and wife
and all
her life
communicating
death
compulsively
to each
who tried
to love her
for herself.

Bright star
unable
to believe
her beauty
or her splendor
or her promise.

From what far
galaxy
does she
look down
in wonder
and regret?

Such a Tide

For low this tide
reveals the sunken
shells and shards
unspoken and concealed
the wreckage of
our journeys
and our goals
the soul's remembrance
of the misbegotten
and the least forgotten
sandstruck
waterlogged
encasement of distaste
and the parched hunger
for the redeeming fish
to swim through all
the waters of our blood.

Re-Entry

The circuit riders are gone. Their successors
are planted not always by streams of living
waters. Their leaf is withered by dryness
within and without and, at times, above,
and their manna is rationed for Sundays.

Who then shall come and knock on my door because
the doorbell is out of order as much
as I and ask how my constitution
withstands the amendments of time and the new
interpretations of change? Who shall appraise
the health of my soul or whatever serves
as soul in my scheme of psychological
structure?
    "Sit down. Sit down," I say. For no one
has shifted personal stance enough for long
to sit where I sit and dangle
ten toes in my shoes and wonder what arrows
are hidden beneath my flesh. "Sit down. Sit down.
And do not tell me but listen. Listen
even when I am silent. Listen even
when I am speaking in tongues not of humans
or of angels but of the shadowy
devils that drug and depress me and drag
me down to my dark and original sense."

There is no incense now to lift our prayers.
They smoulder scentless and deodorized,
sterile against all hints and gestures of faith.
The sky is a carousel for astronauts.
Our craft has pierced the ancient face of God.
We ignore the blood of the crucifixion
which rains as silently as atomic
fallout upon the anemic places
beneath while our geiger counters record
only our brittleness and our imbalance.

Give us a number—any number will do—
and feed us into a mathematical
machine with a better memory than God
had for us or we for God or each other.
We shall be classified and declassified
after we have endured the swish and swash
which neither cleanses nor heals. We come out right—
not really right but right where we started,
trying hard to remember our number
when what we need most of all is a name.
Can God remember our name?

Good God! Or is good a libeling label,
an exclamation of our mutual
indifference—or a double zero we place
to stress our view of the naught of the ought,
the minimal likelihood of there being
a Cause with eyes, a Being begetting
all being? It doesn't compute. It figures
if we are to figure at all. Our silly
caricatures of God have confused us
because we ourselves have been caricatured
by the gods we engraved to displace
the Source of our being.

The circuit riders are still in orbit.
Our raillery and our railing are naked.
We are incinerated but not destroyed.
There is yet the promise of re-entry.

Without a Question Mark

oh what is . . .
oh what is the use
are the words that I heard
of a woman. The noose

of an ought
and a naught
was tightening round
the neck of her mind
though her feet were not
sprung off the ground.

oh what yes . . .
oh what is the know
the hand constantly draws
from the bow

while the unquivered
arrow affirms
life
in wingable terms

Under the Sign of Thomas

Under the sign of Thomas
we live—we doubters—
we wonderers—we wanderers—
scrupulously suspicious
of human and inhuman
dogmatisms,
unfootnoted creeds
and facile suppositions.
We must put
our heads as well as our fingers
at the point where facts
puncture the flesh
and measure how far
love can unsafely go.

My Names Are Different

I am the person you have often met
and, meeting, wonder where you met before.
Familiar as the usual alphabet,
as natural as two and two makes four.

My names are different and my address
varies with all the towns that gave me birth.
The duplicates of me are numberless.
There is a circle of me around the earth.

Hard to believe when I am only I
that others like me live in other places,
while circumstance declines to satisfy
my curiosity to see their faces.

This has been going on for centuries:
men with the same matrix as my being,
my tribe of twins—with separate memories—
whom I must die without so much as seeing.

To See and Follow

O God
my one good eye
less than I wish
and more than I deserve
light of my body
better that it be
single than full
of fumbling darkness.
Use it as me
to see whatever
beauty and truth
You most desire.
Help me respond
to my perceptions
with such faithfulness
that one be good as two
which work as one—
or even with none
I nonetheless be given
to see and follow
even in the dark
your way and will for me.

A Light to Bring Us Safe

Because I live alone
I leave a light
to help me find my way
back home by night.
But if I could
walk home again with you,
to bring us safe
the smallest star would do.

How Do You Patch Your Faith?

How do you patch your faith—she craved—
when you've no coverlet—
or summon bird to sing of hope
with no perch for his feet?

How do you face the unruly hours
which tremble, sway, and blur—
or answer a desire for rain
upon your cheek once more?

And how deliver love's fond word
when boundaried by bed—
aggrieved by unredeemed routine—
by suffering surfeited?

She asks—I too would ask—and yet
she answers in resolve
and saying *Yes* to death and life
with her invincible love.

The tie that binds: two cousins whose fathers are identical twins

IV

Ascendants and
Descendants

Ascendants

I walk up the stairs
and visit with your relatives.
Most of them didn't know me.
Some of them never knew you.
I am glad they are there
in pictures that we pass
and greet
or glance at
or in haste ignore.
Some oval
but some rectangular
and further framed
by the blue and purple
flowers of the paper
you chose for our ascent
and our descent.
Much better that they share
our daily footsteps
than be consigned
to fusty closet shelves
or squirrel-strewn attic nooks
or stacks in a cold garage.
They give the feel
of family
and history past to present
and unterminated
memory and love.

My Mother's Jewelry Box

I am looking for my mother's jewelry box—
casket they would have called it once—not casque
(see helmet) nor cask (see barrel) but something with locks
and a plush interior among whose contents I ask
Why this? Why that? Why did you choose such trinkets
which nothing can rhyme with distinctly, nothing can save—
these rings, this pendant, this watch that will not bear watching?
Ordinarily I associate a casket with a grave.
But this says something of you—a woman—my mother—
stones that are living and colors which warm and shine
when light is upon them and flesh. One after another
I draw them up from your precious and private mine.
I would think I would want to leave them all together
but you would desire them scattered among the young—
your granddaughters, wives of your grandsons, but not this
     evening.
The love of you is in my heart and on my tongue
with no one to tell except myself and—if you are listening—
you who planted them here through the jewelled years—
amethyst, chrysoprase, and diamonds glistening
and sapphires and rubies, and pearls which encase my tears.

My Father's House

My father's house is underground.
There is no door or stair.
There is no light. There is no sound.
Perhaps he is not there.
More space, more time, in the wide sky,
more room for such as he.
For under earth he cannot lie
who holds the stars for me.

Celebration of Love

When they wanted to bury my father the snow
wouldn't let them. It was the spectacular kind of storm
that keeps people at home or at church or wherever
they are when the flakeout comes. His particular norm
was a blizzard back in eighty-eight he remembered
so many times that I lost count. He compared
always with that one and none could ever approach it
even this blockbuster and roadstopper he now shared.
What did it really matter except in terms
of the numbers and comfort of those who desired to come
to say they were glad he had traveled this far safely?
There are times one needs an excuse for feeling numb.
And white is a wonderful color in such a frolic
for one who has seen so much good weather and bad.
Knowing that nothing can finally barricade us
from love, I looked out and knew it would make him glad.

Last Rites

I must memorize
this house
with my eyes

I who grew
with it
I who knew

every square
inch of
wall and stair

Photographs
sure as shutters
only tell us half

Architects'
blueprints are not
visibly correct

when it comes
to measuring
vacuums

filled by folk
who speak no more
as once they spoke

I must climb
these worn stairs
one more time

I must look
through the window
past the brook

I must creep
where the crib
once hedged my sleep

and bend where toys
grew castled cities
for small boys

I must memorize
my old home
with my eyes

and my heart
before machines
crush it all apart

and grade the buried ground
where my first self
I found

A Name

A name is required. To whom are we
indebted and who to us? A name. A name.
But what does a name mean? Derivation
uncertain, always uncertain. Someone
fathered the last name and mothered the middle
and christened the first. I am proud of the name
I was given—given to give to a son
or a book or a star and at last
to a cross or a stone. A name. A name
is required. No number describes me as well.
I can fill out a name, give it muscles
and heart, temper, humor, specifics.
I can give it a face, unique mind-prints
as whorled as my singular fingers.
It compasses me and I it. I shall know
when they call me. A name is required.

Hello, Me

Hello, little boy. Who are you?
Leaning over to sniff the fragrance of that flower
you could be any one of my children,
Tom, Christopher, Jonathan, David,
so close the resemblance.
Who are you?
                Who were you?
                      Who are you?

This is a moment for always:
the shutter has clicked,
the father has taken the picture.
The family keeps everything,
and when the film is developed,
they will keep this too.
Evermore that little boy smelling of the flower
breathing the wonder and the fragrance
of a world which will grow ever larger and more marvelous.

What continuity is there between us?
If I had not been told, I would not know—or believe—
that this is my picture.

I cannot remember when it happened.
I shall never forget that it did happen
because I know now for sure that I was a little boy once
and that at times I can be like a little boy again.

Little boy, smelling of the flower forever,
turn now and look at me. Say:
"Hello. It is good to have been you."

As a Little Child

O Peace of God
as I the child
sleep in the dim church
while the deep Word
surrounds my head
and the heads of my elders.

They are listening
with different ears
and fastening more or less
onto a variety of ideas
each to an own need
and I also.

I also the child
receiving the Kingdom
snug between father and mother
who smile at my slumber
and hearken with new love
to all that this House says.

With Tiny Hands

He has taken away the crèche—
Jon, my baby, my young child,
with his tiny hands and his big basket.
He has taken away the crèche,
the Christmas figures
which I had arranged so carefully
each in the proper position:
the camels . . .
the sheep . . .
the wise men . . .
the shepherds . . .
and Mary . . .
and Joseph . . .
All gone now—
and the Baby too,
the Young Child too.
Taken where he can arrange them for himself
and make his own Christmas—
my baby, my young child—
his very own Christmas.

My Son

My son—another person, me not me—
does not know I see him as much as eyes can see.

Alone in his boat, bent to his thoughts, he rows straight as he can,
with and against the current, by and around the breeze. Boy
    almost man.

Leaves, a thousand crazy pendulums in the active air,
frame my picture of him but hide me there.

Unexpected he came; I was not waiting for him. The sound
of oarlocks, squeaking, too dry, announced there was someone
    around.

Not staring at trees as I but looking into his own private heart
and back where he had traveled from. Not sad, not hurt.

I would have called, wanted to call, but waited to know
if he would see, speak, stop, even let me row.

Farther. Out of sight now. No communication. No sign
we had been near to one another. Still very much my son. Mine.

Our Mutual Friend

We are alone together
    in the liberated house
        and I am much too occupied
            to stroke your fur to make you sing.
You are too individual to accept me
    beyond my ability to open
        cans of cat food
            and doors that will not swing.

Still you would scramble and jump or lie
    on my bed if I were willing to invite you—
        not because you entertain affection
            or admiration or camaraderie
for me. I am only the father
    of your friend who has gone to college
        without translating to you
            the knowledge of your loss or its rationality.

They would not let you matriculate.
    There is no category there for your kind,
        no purpose for your archetypal wisdom,
            so you must stay behind with me and share
the savage silence of a house without him.
    And each of us must find some fantasy
        and curl in dreams and ponder our malaise
            and listen for his step upon the stair.

A Father to Me

He is a virtual father to me
explaining patiently how a house hangs
from a ceiling of stars, how a level
insures the floors and the window casings
and the doors in punctual perspective.
He deciphers the optimal mixture
for the cellar's slab and the cedar texture
for the shingles on the gambrel roof slope.
The lighting fixtures respond to his wit.
The stairs climb in his measured progression.
Under the eaves he hides a tuning fork
for the clean air—and a long luggage rack
for bandboxes and sea chests and other
trifles and treasures of revels and travels.

He is a virtual father to me.
He is willing to answer my questions
and to analyze my observations
and even accepts my contributions.
Instructed by his creativity
I grow in maturity and insight.
I would like to be like him in making
a home so conscientiously constructed
that it might serve as a fit dwellingplace
for unforeseeable generations.

He is a virtual father to me—
my son, the craftsman, the master builder.

Home

Suspend in space
this wall of house
this window out
this threshold in
this roof to tent us
from the night

Precarious
abyss below
or islanded
in fog and wave
dependent on
dim stars
and fragile love

Tom and Dorothy Carlisle on their fiftieth wedding anniversary (photo by Mark Holberg of the Watertown Daily Times)

V

Rise Up, My Love,
My Fair One

Keepsake

This stone
you picked up on the beach
and gave me with a tender smile that said:
Some day, perhaps, I'll want to give you more,
more of my heart, more of my life, my love—
but this will do for now.

And I
held it fondly for a moment,
then slipped it in my pocket, and I kissed you,
not saying, but meaning, in answer to your smile,
the thoughts that pulsed through all my kindled joy:
Some day, perhaps, we'll both be ready for it.
. . . And then we kissed again.

I did not lose the stone.
I have it yet where I can find it when I choose.
The white vein still runs through it, naturally,
for stones don't change, not in a box of keepsakes.
They might, of course, carried in someone's pocket
wear smoother, let us say, or on a shore
or under a glacier or beneath a brook.

But lovers change,
and many a passionate prediction is forgotten.
But you and I did not forget.
Not you.
Not I.
Not ever.

This New Word

You in your own time were given to me
as one created, waiting, then possessed
when time was ready. Essentially
this is what happens again. And all for the best
too—best time, best meaning for unclocked days,
best hope, best love. For me of all men you
the natural divinity for my praise.
I know this now as originally I knew.
But knowing surely cannot take the place
of saying—not as regularly as the chime
sounds its opinion—but with wilder grace
both at an expected and an unexpected time
in terms exactly like none ever heard.
And that is why I bring you this new word.

The Little Girl You Were

Introduce me to her,
child in the photograph,
the little girl you were.
I almost hear her laugh
at the box camera's click,
pleasingly skeptical
of its immortal trick—
your bright original.

Plaid ribbon in her hair
and joy within her head.
I wish I had been there.
Tell me the words you said.
Tell her who she became.
Explain the years of growth
and that she took my name.
Then let me kiss you both.

The Sands of Dawn

You on the beach bending
to choose that shell
that glaciered stone
that sculptured stick
or trace that track
of pipered bird
or the child's castle
and muddy moat
in the sands of dawn.
You whom I love
and choose
for all mornings
and all midnights.

In the Garden

Good Friday in the rain
and darkness over
all the land
this afternoon
but you
risk the unfriendly drizzle
and the premature
and eerie twilight
to plant your peas
the day your father did
for early resurrection
and fruition.

November Night

Late on this November night you rake
leaves which, however arranged, will lie in snow.
You do it for some deep tidiness' sake
and for the heart's exercise, although you know
leaves will not stay where you put them any more
than thoughts. And all this harvest of your arm
is what helps you to get through to the core
of order and harmony. These tines can charm
a science within and beyond your reach
which yearfall and nightfall and love combine to teach.

New Bride

For long in quiet watching
I lie in adoration
of that celestial beauty
that marks her face. I see
composed in living marble
my lovely sleeping lady
who by a grace and goodness
at last belongs to me.

In the Thousand Islands

I think the little isles were made
for wandering winds to whisper to.
Were I the wind and you an isle
I'd always whisper just to you.

My Song of Songs

Watching for the word
to launch the image
of our interminable love
I dream and you
are the enabler
of all my dreams,
the advocate
of all my hopes:
my Eve
my first and only bride,
my Sarah
companion of all my journeys,
my Ruth
whom I entreat
never to leave me,
my Abishag
keeping me alive and warm
despite the years,
and intrinsically
and ecstatically
my Song of Songs.

Every Time and Every Where

For you are fair, my love. Yes, you are fair
and all the years add only to your grace.
My love is every time and every where.

You are the remedy to my despair.
Night disappears when I can see your face
for you are fair, my love. Yes, you are fair.

Of time's tall sum I would not be aware
since days with you provide their own sweet pace.
My love is every time and every where.

You were the answer to my childhood prayer.
That joy no circumstances can erase
for you are fair, my love. Yes, you are fair.

You taught me how to love and how to care.
Because you give me scope and grant me space
my love is every time and every where.

And so today again I would declare
my ecstasy in your renewed embrace
for you are fair, my love. Yes, you are fair.
My love for you is every time and every where.

Rise Up, My Love, My Fair One
(Boaz's Song to Ruth)

Rise up, my love, my fair one. Come away.
The winter of my witlessness is past.
My concentration on the harvest may
have made me heedless but I see at last.
The mist that filmed my mind is over, gone.
The fairest of flowers appears and it is you.
The singing in my heart has me undone
and I am glad and now know what to do.
The figs have ripened. Vines are in full bloom.
Their fruit and fragrance are as naught to all
your luxury which floods away my gloom
and makes me more than eager for your call.
Arise, my love, my fair one. Come away.
This day of days shall be our wedding day.

Ad Infinitum

Love does not end
as all else must,
does not surrender
to the storm or to the dust,
endures although endangered,
wounded yet will heal,
adamant as diamonds,
stubborn as steel.

Beatitude window featuring Emily Dickinson in the Gunnison Memorial Chapel, St. Lawrence University, Canton, New York

VI

The Woman with the Perfect Word

Emily Dickinson

The daffodil she sent to me
arrived a century late.
The calling card she smuggled in
lies on my hallway plate
while through my residence resounds
the tiptoe of delight:
the woman with the perfect word
demure as dynamite.

Since Emily Was Fond of God

Since Emily was fond of God
and God was fond of her,
God let her touch crown jewels
and stare in hidden drawers
aware that secrets she might tell
would fervently require
the password of the hungry child
in search of food and fire.

Restoration

Deprived of faith and love and hope
she bravely built her own
from bees and bluebirds, sunsets, skies
and winds divinely blown.
Re-definition was her stance
and words her instrument
for probing death and life and chance
and all that meaning meant.

Emily Dickinson and the "Burglar"

Some say she raged at God—
no more than Job with his disdain
for the divine injustices
no logic could explain.

Her ire illuminates wry doubts,
Her whimseys make us smile
to find that God enjoys her jokes,
applauds her pique and bile.

To know a Friend so intimate
audacity forgives.
Provocative conversations
are love's prerogatives.

"Mine by the Right of the White Election"

Silence, asylum, suicide—
none such could be her choice
exulting in the pride and power
of her poetic voice.

Lonely—perhaps—but confident
of her identity
who "split the lark" with scalpel deft
left it alive and free.

She leaned against a friendly sun
and tilled the willing earth
and baked the bread of pungent taste
persuaded of the worth

of words arranged in privacy
and ordered to convey
the genius of her generous heart
past resurrection day.

Emily Dickinson and Her "Burglar, Banker, Father"

Because her world averred that God
was super super *man*
she teased *Him* for the arrogance
of patriarchal plan
secure in art of metaphor
to puncture   pierce   impale
errors of partiality
so slanted to the male

The Handwriting of Emily Dickinson

Typography cannot convey
the idiosyncrasy
her pen employed enjoyed and left
for immortality.

The frequent dash which might connote
a plural of intent,
the capitals that crowned and marked
her globe and firmament.

The letters formed as fast to catch
the message that her mind
received by cosmic telegraph
or tireless wireless wind.

Characters of her literacy
almost illegible
but ardent to delight excite
and dynamite the dull.

A Miser's Privilege

If I possessed a manuscript
that Dickinson once wrote,
a poem on a paper bag,
a friendly flower note
or even envelope addressed
in her surprising hand,
I would not part with it for pearls
or diamonds or bonds.

I might bequeath to public place
the treasure that I prize
or let them photograph it now
for other loving eyes,
but to surrender while I lived
would seem a sacrilege—
epitome of selfishness
a miser's privilege.

In Manuscript
(Emily Dickinson)

Give me the manuscript. Permit me
to pore over the choice wealth
of alternative words. The nuances
are dependent on associations
and experiences—private—peculiar.
The heartbeat—the pulse rate—
vary with each loving scholar.
Mine may be as accurate as any.
The author is beyond our bafflements.
Despite all idiosyncrasies
we hold in quivering fingers
a decipherable treasure
a legacy of incandescence.

Before the Guests Arrive

When I think of Emily Dickinson
starving in a mansion
for friends to share her banquet,
patient but anguished
for an authentic audience,
I wonder who
now and where
will die before the guests
arrive for dinner.

Window to World

The stained-glass window strives to enshrine
the woman for our eyes
with colors luminous and apt,
artifacts she would prize,
and hints of her accomplishments
we wisely celebrate.

We cannot leave her there alone,
confined and isolate,
but let her leap to waiting arms
and lips that love to speak
and catch intensity of her lines—
the powerfully meek
who makes the name of Dickinson
with Emily attached
a gift of hidden gold and jewels—
a treasury unmatched.

    The window here described is found in the Gunnison Memorial Chapel at St. Lawrence University, Canton, N.Y.

Well-Versed
(Commentary on Poem #1078
by Emily Dickinson)

You feared that Emily believed
love could be put away—
the heart swept up—not used again—
on any earthly day.

Imprisoned in your cell of pain
without your books for play
your nimble memory retrieved
words that the poet made

and cried against the unwarranted
dismissal of life's last
betrayal—love's retirement—
all its employment past.

You could not summon earlier lines
which labeled death the date
and only then relinquishment
of love's esteemed estate

and only for a season stored
in a convenient drawer
awaiting that most gracious time
when death shall be "no more."

Evening at Peggy's Cove in Nova Scotia, Canada

VII

On the Shores
of Nova Scotia

Necessary Maintenance

You sketch
the lighthouse
and the wave
the cove
the wharf
the electric sky
to save them
for some inland day.
I watch the gulls'
itinerant play
and listen
to their foreign phrases
from fish-store roof
and tide-washed rock.
That island
seems a world
away
and Paddy's Head
projects its prominence
around the curve
of blue St. Margaret's Bay.

We wish—
oh how we wish—
that we could stay
and draw
from what we see
and taste
and touch
and smell
and hear
the peace we need
to buoy
and shore us up
until another year.

Returning

Again and again
we returned
through the clouds
through the air
dripping with sea
walked back
to the weathered
wharf and waited
for the fog
to raise
our spirits

We chatted
like gulls
at home
on the gradual
tide our feathers
matted by mist

Tomorrow
the sun
or the next day
or ever
to cut
the mystery
with a bright
knife spreading
our catch
to dry
and be counted
incredibly
edible
and succulent
and satisfying

Voyager

The foghorn
focuses the rock
and waves the sailor
past the treacherous reef.
What signal
guides my tortured course
to bring me safe to joy
past all my pain
ingratitude and grief
to harbors bright with grace
and the long longed-for Face?

A Taste for Tempest

Ocean contrives
a nonchalance
when seas are calm
and winds at rest.
I think I like
its passion best
when the wild whitecaps
swirl and dance.

Yet were I sailor
in storm's shock
my prayer might
desperately be
for some polite
serenity
to set me safe
past reef and rock.

A Metaphor for All Who Love the Sea
(Peggy of Peggy's Cove, Nova Scotia)

Little did Peggy know, the night the storm
smashed the small schooner on the rock-high coast
and swept the seamen out and down and down
till all but she were lost
and miracle past miracle the waves
transported her soaked body to the shore
where strong and tender cove-folk pulled her safe,

that she would live in lore
a metaphor for all who love the sea
yet know its grisly terror and frenzied fame
and, praying protection, fervently recall
her rescue and her name.

Good Morning

The wharf is empty but the sun-risen cove
is calling the tide and day is calling me.
A cordial cat brushes my leg, comes back
to say *Good Morning* and to smell the sea.

A sandpiper, ignoring all I am,
tiptoes in haste across these weathered planks.
The gulls come crying for some sustenance.
Nourished as I have been, I offer thanks.

Invitation

You do not need to ask the shore
to spread its arms to take you in.
Lovers are less available,
more ignorant of what might have been.
Here all you have to do is lie
at length and hear the sea gulls cry
and watch the little boats go by.
You and the sea are close of kin.

Beacon

I thought I saw the lighthouse raise
its special sunlight from the rock.
The mist obscured the interval.
Waves pounded, foaming, shock on shock.

How can I chart my journey home
unless past my anxiety
a light defines the path I take
and brings me safely through the sea?

Ship-Fellow

In our wake
he waits
with the sea gulls
and the great whales
and all the small creatures
of the distant deep.

He walks also
before us
where the waves
wait for such comers
and cry *Hallelujah*
at his light.

And oh!
past the unseeing
portholes
of our faring
he fellow-ships
with us.

Personal Geology

Sandstone,
granite,
schist—
this is my rocky list.
The sediment of youth,
the igneous cooled by age,
the metamorphic truth—
my total heritage.

Hibernative

In the long winters I repeat
the words I hear from travelers
who stop to chat in summer's heat.

Silence at length can be a curse
though a brief blessing well I know
when it defines my universe.

I wish they did not have to go
and stay away through all this cold
and quiet prison of the snow.

So in those welcome weeks I'm bold
to talk and urge their talk with me.
It is my season of panning gold

to tide me through monotony
with the bright glows of memory
while I sit lonely by the sea
without a shred of company.

Girders spanning a bridge near New York

VIII

Part of a Purpose

People Part of a Purpose

Back in those forests we walk—
Connecticut, Massachusetts—
wondering whether we
could have made it
in Newtown
in Hartford
Northampton
or Northfield
so hard it was
to be a beginner
with no insurance
or assurance
their efforts would take.

While they were huddling
in hope of spring
in scanty heat
from the logs of the land
they had cleared
and were eager to sow
and to harvest,
they remembered
the Children of Israel
wandering wildernesses
of sand and sun.
They confessed their faith
that their land was as promised
and fertile and fruitful
as that which Joshua conquered
in the book they obeyed.

Sometimes they buried
more of their children
than grew to be parents themselves.

They married again
when husband or wife
succumbed to the rigors
they shared. They must—
they knew they must—
look forward and forward and forward.

Sometimes it meant
starting again upriver
uprooting, re-routing,
making new maps for the land,
new laws for their misunderstandings,
a meetinghouse for their prayer
and a new God's Acre
to set their stones of remembrance.

From those stones and the records
their clerks inscribed and preserved
we trace—or the diligent trace—
the lines of our lineage.

We discover a William
or several Williams,
a John or a Lemuel or Luther
or Samuel
and wonder where we
would have been without them.

There were maiden names too
as memorable as Mary
and Abigail and Bethiah
and Lydia and Betsy
Tryphena and Elizabeth
or whatever the appellations
of the saints
and occasional sinners—
our precursors who blessed us
by being, begetting and bearing
and persevering—

persevering, enduring—
and making their valorous imprint
bequeathing more than their wills
could catalog or devise—
more than the fields and the dwellings
and the cloaks and the scarves and the petticoats
and the warming pans and the skillets
and the candlesticks and the kettles
and the featherbeds and the bolsters
and the butter tubs and the barrels.

Outright they gave—we inherit—
their spunk and some of their spirit.
Recover their story
as best we can and savor
the salt and the spice and the sweetness
and cherish—most gratefully cherish—
their vigor, their foresight, their faith.

Whichever their names
we are beholden
we relative offspring
of old and new England
we are beholden
and looking back to their greatness,
their enterprise, their initiative,
we find the force to go forward,
the impulse to persevere
here with our pains and our problems
large but not larger than theirs.

People part of a purpose
that did not begin and must not
conclude with us. We promise
and pledge our lives to that promise.

Domestic Correspondence
Two Days before Bunker Hill

"Courage we have," wrote Abigail
that June which followed Lexington
and posted by the uncertain mail
of traveling friend to husband John.
Abundant courage, she declared,
and conduct too we shall not want.
But powder for the stand they dared
was far too precious and too scant.

Her letter closed with a request—
as simple as a cask of sand,
she realized, but she was pressed—
for pins. If any were at hand
in Philadelphia the price
ten times what it had been before
would still be worth the sacrifice
if John could find them in some store
and put them in his trunk so she
could have them some reunion day.

Powder and pins and bravery:
Their patriot war was won that way.

From the Grave of a Revolutionary Soldier at Williamsburg

One sleeve-link left and half of a second,
two arms the man had before he was buried
in the cemetery in the garden
of the Palace of the Governor
in Williamsburg after Virginia
seceded from England.
     The Governor left
while there was time, knowing the choler
of those who thought liberty preferable
to life. So count the dissolved soldier
a Virginian, an American.
     Look for
more than a sleeve-link, some buttons perhaps,
pewter or bone sewn on a uniform.
Do not expect to discover
a uniform now, as unrecoverable
as the heart of this bearer of arms
and of sleeve-links.
     This clay pipe
may have been his or may have belonged to
the grave digger; and this pottery
must be the work of an Indian
long before English folk ventured
to share the land by the James—
or whatever the Indians called it.

The knife blade, the buckle, the key
are attributable to the soldier,
his dignity, his possession, even en route
to the grim ground in the gay garden.
No lock inhibits the shovel.
No need now for the key, the buckle, the knife.

And the nails, the handwrought spikes of iron
sieved through the soil of time
and drawn by no magnet of dust:
nails from his coffin or nails in his pocket?
Nailed him in briefly at most,
no wood for their teeth now.

Sift the artifacts gently. No disrespect
is intended. We are respectable
grave robbers, looking for heroes and history.
Finger this bullet. Perhaps he
carried it in his equipment. Perhaps it
prefaced his progress to death and severed
a sleeve-link while uncoupling him.

Sign Here

Safe under glass this Declaration lies
of Independence of a bygone age.
We read the words again with grateful eyes,
remembering the numerous Julys
since they inscribed their names upon this page.

That we may prove again there is no dearth
of freedom lovers, come, unlock this shrine.
That freedom may not perish from the earth,
lift up this contract of our nation's birth,
and where they signed their names we, too, shall sign.

A Severe Struggle

It is a severe struggle
to be certain of our alignment
in past revolutions
and experiments.
So much to be said
for being safe
rather than brave
or for feeling approved
rather than being accurate
in our diagnosis
of the right road
for the right cause,
and the real conscience.
We face the same
torment and misgivings
in the struggle to certify
our current stance
and allegiance.
It has never been easy.

Re-Crossing Brooklyn Ferry
(*with Walt Whitman*)

I shall cross Brooklyn Ferry with you, Walt—or the Bridge
    if the Ferry isn't running—
and ask you to show me how in my century and in heaven's name
I can praise such a bestial city, such a brutal city,
    your Manhattan, your Brooklyn,
a city where boys and girls before they are adolescents are bums
    or whores or drug addicts or drunks or criminals,
whose tenements no longer give hope of a rise in the world
    to something cleaner, better, and free of poverty,
whose buildings are fouled and grimed and gritted,
    obscene and obnoxious and noxious.
Even the waters underneath this prow, this thoroughfare,
    are so damnably and permanently polluted
that the stench is more than my stomach can stand.
I cry for the breeze to relieve me of this garbage,
    this grotesque incense
lifting its redolence to a godless sky
    and invoking no celestial apparatus.

But you would call me comrade, friend, and convert my savage
    spleen to ecstasy.
You would speak to me of the brave and beautiful skyline
    which even the Babel towers conspire to create.
You would speak to me of museums, parks, universities,
    hospitals,
    warehouses of good will.
You would extol the neighborhood delicatessen,
    the ice-cream shop with more flavors than anyone
    could ever get around to purchase.
You would say I should visit Shea Stadium and see how the Mets
    shape up for the coming season and how their faithful fanatics
    achieve conviviality.
You would show me the firefly patterns of traffic by night,
    like spider-lace in their intricacy.

You would celebrate the offices of book publishers
        and magazine editors,
    of exporters and importers of an infinite variety
    of practical and beneficial products.

You would sing of people, people, people
        who look you in the face
    and call you by your "nighest name."
You would show me how your America would be
        like a castrated giant,
    an amputated athlete, if this royal city, this holy city,
    your Manhattan, your Brooklyn, were to be destroyed
    and the place thereof should know it no more.

Walt, my brother, you promised to share this crossing
        with men and women
    of a generation or of ever so many generations hence—
    fifty years, a hundred years, or ever so many hundred years.
That is why I invoke your spirit and recall you from Valhalla.
That is why I claim your wisdom, your vision,
        your undiscourageability,
    your faith in people and cities, and your enthusiasm
    for the democratic program and process.

"You furnish your parts toward eternity
. . . you furnish your parts toward the soul."

Hosannas in the Forest
(Albert Schweitzer)

The children of the forest
sang shrill hosannas
in their own pitch and language
when he came to bury
himself among them.

He tore out his eyes,
he broke off his fingers,
and gave them willingly
that the operation
might be successful.

The secret of the Messiah
he shared—the supper
all day long and far
into the evening
and across the jungle.

Organs responded
as he fought manually
to restore tone
and tissue.
He kept in practice.

Pelican, pig,
antelope, crocodile,
flower, and son of man
were all prey
to his reverence.

The execution
of his commitment
screamed HALT!
to the castration
of humanity.

Remembering Hiroshima
and Nagasaki

O God
Your breath
is in us.
There is no
life without You.
Yet we know too well
how to destroy
the breath
and life
of others.
From fist
to knife
to nuclear bomb—
by paying
no mind
no heart—
we know too well
how to destroy
the breath
and life
of others.

Forgive us.
Heal us.
Help us sing Your praise.
And curb our insolence
which authors and exacts
Your anger.

Like Cain
we do not comprehend
the blood we shed
the breath we stifle—

or contrive
to implement
or to ignore
the stifling.

We have not learned
to mourn for others
in the generous way
we pity and excuse
ourselves.

Come, O come
Emmanuel
and heal us
and Your other children.
Speak Peace.
Empower us also
to speak Peace
both near and far
throughout
Your threatened earth.   *Isaiah 57:14-19*

Destruction to the Nth Power

I read somewhere about a wooden
horse rolled into an ancient city
as though it were some magnificent
gift, some new and invigorating god,
some savior contemptuous of all
enemies and able to cremate
any who doubted its deity.

And I know it is not then but now.

A Matter of Morals

Jonah would not have killed
one Ninevite directly.
He was too sober
too responsible
too upright
for that kind
of murder.
But he did not flinch
from wishing megatons
to fell them all.
No ethical
or moral
issue he could see
would be involved.
It seemed a sober
and responsible
and upright
kind
of act.

Build Me a Shelter

A cave is to come out of. Underground
is temporary. We were made to breathe
star-laughter and the breeze's latest word.
Security is solid but not sweet.
Freedom's main chance is running in the sun
not buried waiting for a global ruin
more hellish than the medieval image
of hell. Build me a shelter
above ground and in sight of sky and wide
to kinship with the world's diversity.

America Dawn

Out of the dawn
the American cities
rise
      pure
             and white
even their smoke
like colorless vapor
easing over the rooftops
like a sheltering tent
a benevolent benediction
ensuring the sleep
and the safety
of all beneath.
It is a beautiful
picture from the late
late train arriving now
or the all-night bus
or the coastal plane
circling to set down
beside it. The city
I say is beautiful
reverent
austere
steeped in centuried memories
its buildings like monuments
raised in the burial ground
and reminding its people
of titans who labored
and entered in
to their labors
and left
a cryptic message
of what their industry
means in the new horizons.

They fail to guide us
clearly. They know
dawn's pristine ecstasy
grows gradually grayer
till soot and smoke
and daily deposits of other
effluvia and excrement
turn day's reveille
to a dark and urgent dirge.
It is not fair we say.
Our original dream
is sataned
by the sin
of millions
of greedy fingers
producing
becoming products
consumed and being consumed
wasting and being wasted
by forges, assembly lines
the beat and the belch
and the automatic
mountain of goods—
we call them good
in the plural—
piled high against
the sky of our future.

It is hot and noon—
No—long past noon
and the evening
offers no natural promise
redeeming our Babel.
This shining city
of painted wood
and cracked concrete
and iron and stained steel
cries for cool tunnels
or bathyscaphe depths

or orbits of moons
or an Eden planet
for a second start
and hope
for bombed-out memories
of the despicable knowledge
of how to despoil
and desecrate.

And yet
the day waits again.
I feel it as the artist-
conductor comments:
My city beautiful
he says at dawn—
and someday maybe later—
but at dawn how white
how hopeful how clean
even the air refreshed
from some higher reserve
while the busy and tired
were resting against their will—
my city the beautiful.
The bus driver smiles
at his terminal
and the early workers.
The night shift he knows
beats the day by a small margin.
He rejoices to be
within reach of home.
The stewardess yawns
and adjusts to a different
seatbelt politely
inquiring how sunrise
renews you as well
as the city you sink to
with musings of Athens
and Rome and Paris
and London and Brussels

the older the building
the better in retrospect.

But now
       now
           now
                now
purely and simply
it is dawn
world dawn
America dawn
dawn in the city
and the day waits again
uncolored and new
and we know
as we step
down into it
or up into it
or out into it
that seeing these white
monolithic figures
rising from the earth
which holds them with minimum sway
and suspended from heaven
like pendulums of promise
ticking and tocking
with temporal insistence
created from creation
designed by courtesy
of a greater than Euclid.

In retrospect
we almost know
boxed in though we are
conditioned as we may be
in the complex we occupy
our not-so-private compartment
among these totems
and temples

and tombs
we know
there is life
in vision—
the sculpture
that we
and others
can quarry
and carve
the jagged components
of Camelot
or Jerusalem
or even a new Chicago
in this new dawn
this millionth chance
this unconsumed mercy.

A cock is crowing.

A footbridge in southern Vermont

IX

Our Jeopardy

Our Jeopardy

It is good
to use
best china
treasured dishes
the most
genuine goblets
or the oldest
lace tablecloth
there is a risk
of course
every time
we use anything
or anyone
shares an inmost
mood or moment
or a fragile
cup of revelation
but not to
touch not to
handle not to
employ the available
artifacts of being
a human being
that is the quiet
crash the deadly
catastrophe
where nothing is ever
enjoyed or broken
or spoken or spilled
or stained or mended
where nothing is ever
lived
loved
pored over
laughed over
wept over
lost
or
found

Through Cross Country

It is a long race
across more country
than we can vision,
more fields than we can
sow, more brooks than we
can watch fill up with rains.

We must learn to pace
ourselves. This is no
short dash, so many meters
or yards and then
over and the short breath
sooner to normal. This
is measured in components
of centuries.

One ingredient is grace,
though the cup for that
sometimes fills slowly
drop by crystal drop
before it runs
over or dry
or past us.

None are permitted to retrace
the hill behind
to locate the untaken
turn. This clock
cannot be wound
backwards or its hands
reshuffled.

No resting place
is provided except
in the new country
beyond the crack
of dawn, where weary
runners have new
legs and new eyes.

When Age Enmeshes Me

When age enmeshes me
God grant that I may see,
God grant that I may hear
and that my mind be clear,
my tongue in good control
and springtime in my soul.

Retrieval System

In this ripe brain I store
my pyramids of facts,
pages of poems, lore
of peaks and cataracts,
wild wonderings and staid
conjectures and dark dreams
and treasures unassayed
and embryonic themes.
I trust the tenuous
computer memory
to guard its impetus
while years devour me.
What waste that I can't stash
these assets past the day
my psychic atoms smash
and I am hid away.

Requisition

I ask the long
afternoon to linger
puttering as I do
with flowers
and words
and dreams.
The tide
tells its time
and mine must be
sychronized
to fit its flow.
I know the night
must come.
I hope it waits
till I complete
my song.

Almost Inaudible

The house was empty of all sounds but hers
and the sounds a house has as years go by.
I came to listen for the whirr she heard,
for rustle, hum, hiss, or muffled sigh.
She was positive anyone with ears
could recognize the motor near the arch
behind the plaster and along the wall.
The wind outside the window mentioned March
as the likely month. Splatter of giant
snowflakes on the pane promised that spring
was all around waiting for an entrance.
Still she kept listening, listening
for footsteps, sobs, soughs, whispering shadows
that appeared when she was by herself.
No one else could find a door unbolted,
cobweb parted, dust disturbed on any shelf.
She had heard and seen something. I believed her
even if they didn't but I closed the door
since ghosts have a genius for proliferating.
I have enough myself without inviting more.

Moon Song

"Please, Mr. Moon,
won't you sell?
I need your land.
I need your well.
You could do better
nearer town.
It's hard up here.
It's easier down.
I own the acres
every side.
Your stubborn plot
I can't abide.
I want it
to complete my sphere
of field and farm
and forest here."
But Alfred Moon
would not agree.
Surrounded
in his tenancy
he still preferred
to cut his wood
and grow whichever
crops he could.
Whatever Amos
Hopkins said
he'd see himself—
I quote him—dead
before his pride
and joy he'd sell.
And anyone
could go to hell
who tried to change
his cash-proof mind.

And so upon
the maps we find
to Amos'
blandishments immune
the island owned
by A. C. Moon.

Adelia Moon

Adelia Moon
was tall and lean,
pleasant but quiet,
rarely seen
beyond the farm,
more rarely down
to share the stir
of Williamstown.
When Andrew Jackson
Moon, her spouse,
died of consumption
then the house
and farm were left
to her and son
Benjamin Franklin
Moon (the one
a gunshot wound
put underground).

With Andrew gone
Adelia found
the farm too much
for her alone:
cattle to feed,
crops to be grown
to fill the chilly
cellar store,
the wilderness
kept from the door.

And so it happened
sometime soon
she found herself
another Moon.
A nephew Alfred
son of Dan
married Adelia
and they ran
this mountain farm
the larger part
of fifty years
until his heart
was giving out
and they moved in
with Whitneys—
no one of their kin
but nearer town
and nearer too
where Doctor Nelson
could get through.

Though Alfred died there
before long,
she still remained
and her moon song
continued while
her rocking chair
kept its contented
rhythm there
until, one hundred
three years spent,
to no one's real
astonishment,
reticent and
obedient,
she went without
dispiritment
where Andrew, Ben,
and Alfred went.

The Tragedy of Attrition

What do you do
with old Bibles
old flags
old buildings
old people
after they are worn out
in service
or no longer needed—
for some obscene reason.

Shred them.
Burn them.
Take them down
brick by brick
or wall by wall
in one giant bulldozing.
Quietly contract
diminish
abate
consume
deplete
their strength
their vision
their dignity.

Know that it may
happen to you
that way
some day.

Golden Hour

Let it not come too soon
nor go too soon:
that golden hour
of the afternoon
when what we dreamed
becomes what we recall
and what seemed everything
is whispering, "This is all."

A Touch of Autumn

There comes a day when suddenly summer shivers—
still on the books but marked for a headlong exit;
and I cry for the clock to strike the identical number
over and over and over as though it could know
nothing later
and nothing better
and nothing beyond this sunrise.

As Long as I Can

Sooner or later the frost will come.
This is the season for ending things.
This is the time for harvesting trees
and saying good-by to southbound wings.
Sooner or later the frost will come
for flowers and fruit and ripe desire.
But as long as I can these autumn nights,
I shall gather branches and build a fire.

All Is Safely Gathered

More beautiful than billboards
the weathered barns
leaning and straining
to stand their ground. The slant
carries rain well. The crows
flap by assessing
depreciation. The swallows
are wary of twittering walls.
The mice honeycomb the old hay—
their cushion against crash.
Decay nibbles without headlines
the same as yesterday.

Such senility is eye salve
to others who go down slowly
reminiscing where they were raised.

Isaac and Rebecca

Old Isaac
is not listed
in the census
of 1830.
He lived
so long
a journey
up the mountain
that no one
wanted
to walk up
and ask
his name
and numbers
for the hay
and corn
he grew
and trees
he cut.
He got
left out.
So Isaac's
only entry
is the private
grave that Rebecca
dug and scratched
with stone on stone
to mark the spot
so she
could find it
in the autumn evening.

Prospect

Tomorrow we shall go walking
in the cemetery
and search inscriptions
from a century
before the century
before our own.
These stones have meaning
privately preserved
beside the pasture
on the still hillside.
We shall observe
the chiseled anguish
and the aspirations
of the buriers
who lay down at last
in the same silent space
dwelling forever
in the hand of God.